ALONG THE WAY

My Journey with Horses

KAREN IRLAND

Along The Way: My Journey with Horses

ISBN: 9781688963795

Copyright ©2019 Karen Irland

Front and back cover photos: Courtesy of Epona Moon Photography

Prepress services and book design: Kathleen Weisel (weiselcreative.com)

Books sold in the United States are printed in the United States.

karen.irland1@icloud.com

No rider above, no horse below.

For Maggie –

Best wishes always,
in all of your ventures –
Happy trails,
xx
Karen

To my darling Dad,
Who always encouraged me to follow my dreams.

CONTENTS

Foreword ix

Introduction. xi

In the Beginning. 1

Riding Hunter Jumpers 3

Eventing Years 7

Learning from the Masters 11

Seeking Connection 15

Meeting Sally Swift 17

A Lesson with Sally 21

Teaching 25

Riding and Life 27

Core Truths. 31

Humans are Vertical, Horses are Horizontal 37

Andy. 43

Movement 45

Riding the Crest of the Wave 51

Breath is Life. 53

The Art of Listening. 57

The Eyes Have It! 61

Letting Go 65

Ride the Up 69

Clear Intent. 73

Monkey Mind 77

Through the Reins 81

Slow and Steady 87

Riding Light 91

Being in Partnership 95

And The Journey Continues. 99

In Appreciation 103

Some Good Reads 105

FOREWORD

KAREN IRLAND HAS A DREAM. She dreams that someday, all horseback riders will have the knowledge and the tools to be able to achieve an amazing partnership with their horse. By looking within themselves first and then to their horses, they can develop relationships where their horses are physically able and mentally willing to do the movements that are requested of them.

This is Karen's story. She has ridden horses throughout her life. In the following pages, Karen shares her riding experiences along with the information and guidance of her riding instructors. Through integrating the teachings of Sally Swift with information about the psoas, Karen has enhanced both her own horseback riding and her teaching. She has been able to achieve remarkable results in assisting her riding students to have better relationships and get better movements with their horses..

Karen taught me the concept that horses are horizontal beings and people are vertical beings. Many riding instructors teach their students to follow the horizontal movement of their horses. This results in the students pushing into their horses' backs and actually interfering with their horses' movement. Karen teaches that riding horses is primarily a vertical movement for the rider. By riding vertically, riders get out of the way of their horses, which not only allows the horses to move horizontally but also gives them the opportunity to collect themselves and lift vertically.

Karen is riding her dream and it is her mission in life to share how she does this for the benefit of all riders and horses she meets. I urge you to follow along with Karen as she shares her journey. Learn from her knowledge and experience and then go out and practice to become the rider you have always dreamed of being.

– Tom Nagel, author of *Zen & Horseback Riding*

INTRODUCTION

THIS BOOK IS THE STORY OF MY DISCOVERIES on my riding journey. "*Along The Way*" is truly just what it says, the winding path that I am (still!) traveling to become a better human, horsewoman, and rider. Included are writings from my journal, lessons from my mentors, letters from students, and stories about my own horses. It is about the path of my own search for what all riders want—that elusive perfect partnership with our horses.

The real facts of great riding seem to be a well-kept secret. As students, we are given a lot of difficult, frustrating and often contradicting instructions to 'do this or that' to our horses. We struggle along making little progress. The few, and there are *very* few, natural athletes among us have no aware-ness of 'how they do what they do' on a horse. Unfortunately, this does not make them the best instructors for the average rider!

You may have been told: "Sit *down* in the saddle. Relax! Sit up! Heels down! Put him on the bit! Forward! Quiet hands! Stop bouncing!" Oh so helpful, right? Like me, you were probably doing your best to follow instructions, without a clue as to *how* this was to be done. The result is often frustra-tion for the student and an unhappy horse. Guided by my classical coaches and teachers and helped by body workers in many fields, I have come to a simple truth of effective riding. That is, our primary job as riders, is to learn *how* to use our *own* bodies correctly, both on and off our horses.

Karen Irland and *Andy*, her Haflinger gelding.
Photo courtesy of Epona Moon Photography.

*There can be no 'perfect partnership' with
our horses, unless we take responsibility for
ourselves when we ride. – KI*

The key to this, as we have been told over and over, is in
our seat. But finding our seat, or center, is often misunder-
stood in the riding world. "Sit deep in the saddle, balance
on your seat bones, sit on your pockets," and the many other
directions I was given never helped. Finally, when I met Sally
Swift and discovered my *center* through her techniques, it
was life changing. Next, from Tom Nagel I learned about the
real core muscles of the body, the *psoas*. The psoas muscles
give riders stability in the saddle, while allowing us to ride
with flexibility and balance. This is something that few of us
do in life, let alone when we climb up on our horses' backs,
expecting miracles to happen! There is, of course, more to the
whole riding game. But discovering and learning to ride with
awareness of our true center and our core muscles is the very
important basic beginning to the whole picture of riding well.

The following chapters are the result of my more than
fifty years of riding, including thirty years of teaching. My
students and mentors have encouraged me to "write it down!"
So, here are the experiences that have enabled me, and my
students, to find real success and true partnership with our
horses in a stress free, positive way. They apply to every horse
and every rider, regardless of experience or style. I sincerely
hope that this book will help *you* on your 'riding way.'

– Karen Irland, 2019

In the Beginning

Born with the horse bug.

GALLOPING ACROSS COUNTRY FIELDS as a horse crazy kid is one of my first riding memories. I was very lucky to begin riding when I was young and able to enjoy the delight of simply being with horses. In those days, in central Michigan, there were few fences and plenty of room to roam on a horse. I spent many hours in the saddle, traveling with my equine buddy to every place possible.

I rode my bike to a nearby vegetable farm to work for riding money and every penny I earned went to the local stable. I was the classic horse crazy kid. When I rode, the possibilities were unlimited! On the back of a horse I was completely free to travel, imagine, and escape to wonderful places.

My horse and I tracked deer, jumped logs, or just ambled through the woods. With my horsey friends we raced through fields and woods and swam the horses in the pond. We were Indians, cowgirls, jockeys; you name it. We lived our fantasies on and through our horses. Those years of totally uninhibited riding were a wonderful way to grow up and definitely shaped my life down the road.

Anyone born with the horse bug will identify with this. Horses can teach young people confidence, inner strength and responsibility, and provide good healthy activity that is much needed. (For kids of *all* ages!) For me, horses were also the buffer and the comfort for the trials of life. No matter what was going on at the time, the horses would always make me feel complete and whole when I was with them.

Many years later, I can see that those early years of riding bareback and carefree times gave me a natural seat on a horse. I had no formal instruction in those days and in that I was actually fortunate. I learned to stay centered and go with the horse because it was how I stayed on! Horse time was all about fun and companionship. I did not worry about 'doing' anything at all. I rode for the simple pleasure of just being part of my horse.

Most of us ride because we love horses, and I believe we need to remember this. It is so easy to get wrapped up in the intensity of training and lose perspective. Today, if I find myself getting too serious about my riding, I think about being a kid on a horse again and voilà, problem solved!

Riding Hunter Jumpers

A rider's job is to be invisible, quiet and considerate of her horse.

AT SIXTEEN, I WAS FINALLY OLD ENOUGH to drive a car and expand my horizons. No surprise, my first job was working as a groom in a large A-level hunter barn. It was a fantastic learning experience for a teen. The barn managers were a British couple who practiced the precise horse care that the English are known for. Thanks to them, I learned stable management from the best. The real bonus, however, was being able to ride the resident schoolmasters. It was a privilege to be taught by such high level dressage and jumping horses. Weekly lessons and riding on the outdoor jump course taught me skills that most young people only get in Europe. That time was a priceless part of my horse education.

This experience hooked me on jumping and I soon found my way to the hunter world. My high school and college years were spent training and showing over fences. I loved the process of developing a partnership with my horses and the challenge of a smooth, clean round over fences. Jumping with a horse is an incredible thrill—being airborne, in perfect balance together, is as close to actually flying that one can get.

During those years, I had an excellent coach in Tim Wright, of Stony Creek Farm in Michigan, who schooled me in the art and style of good hunter riding. Tim taught pure, classical hunt seat—a balanced, flowing position over the jumps with soft following hands. No 'crest releases' or balancing on the horse's neck allowed. Hours of lessons without stirrups or reins over jumps and gymnastic grids taught me to depend on my own balance and not use my horse for support. The rider's job was to be invisible, quiet, and considerate of her horse. Tim taught quality of riding over winning ribbons. I can still see his flawless riding position and smooth fluidity, on any horse. He turned out great riders, who in turn, allowed their horses to be their best.

My mounts in those days were mainly thoroughbreds off the track. They had talent and suppleness and made good jumpers—if you could unscramble their race trained minds. I remember going to the track in Detroit, picking out prospects, and taking them home to re-train. This meant hours of patience, tact, and basic flatwork. Those ultra-sensitive horses taught me a lot about taking time with a horse and to ride lightly and considerately. Thoroughbreds are incredible athletes and if you can combine that with patient training, you have a wonderful jumper who will take you over anything. Those were valuable experiences that I still appreciate and I have wonderful memories of my favorite hunters *Mathew* and *Smooth Sailing*.

Bar None at Gladstone, New Jersey.

Eventing Years

Did I give you permission to dismount?

AFTER COLLEGE, I LEFT THE HUNTER WORLD and moved on to eventing, which had just started up in Michigan and was quickly becoming very popular. It was an exciting new sport that had everything! Eventing is like a triathlon and was originally a test for the cavalry. You compete in three different tests of skill and endurance—dressage, cross-country, and stadium jumping phases.

I was hooked! For the next ten years, I traveled throughout the Midwest and East coast to compete. The exciting challenge of riding over all kinds of terrain, at speed and over fences, is a real test for a horse and rider team. The years I spent as an event rider gave me an inner strength and determination that has stayed with me my entire life. The training involved also showed me that we always have just a bit more in us than we think, and that we can accomplish anything if we are willing to work for it.

My best event horses, *Pathfinder* and *Bar None*, were both appendix Quarter horses. They had the ideal combination of speed, strong jumping ability, and great minds. They also had the good sense to collect themselves when facing a steep slope with a ditch at the bottom, or a drop jump into the water, and they had the Quarter horse's strength and agility

Pathfinder

for any task. They were fast and intelligent over the courses, and took me places I never imagined possible. It was truly special to be partnered with those incredible horses.

My mentor and coach in those years was Robert Hutton, BHSI, (British Horse Society Instructor). Bob was a classic horseman who had been in the British cavalry and ridden in the Olympics in his day. He moved to the States after his retirement from the army and coached eventing students at his barn in Metamora, Michigan. His years of training cavalry recruits made him a tough but excellent instructor. From Bob, I learned how to get a horse (and myself!) truly fit through correct, systematic interval training. He taught me the skills needed for each phase of a horse trial; the precision for dressage, how to rate my horse's speed on the courses, ride over different terrain and jumps, and the balance and control required for the stadium jumping phase. From water obstacles and oxers, to ditches and drop jumps, Bob schooled us over every possible situation.

Bob's unique style and his droll, British humor would have me laughing over mishaps and accepting the ups and downs of riding and competing with humor and grace. Looking back, these were life skills that apply to everything. One day, my overly fresh horse decided to buck me off in my cross-country lesson. (Picture me lying on the ground gasping for breath while *Old Dobbin* is making tracks for the barn.) Bob ran up to me, made sure I was OK, then announced in his uppercrust British accent: "Did I give you permission to dismount?" Yep, that was Bob, making a joke to get me past a tough moment!

One of my event horses, *Bar None*, had raced on the track, was very fast and loved to run. Occasionally, we would have the complete, out-of-control runaway during a cross-country lesson. Trust me, being run off with on a real racehorse is a lot different than a gallop on the average saddle horse! After one of these runaway incidents, and what seemed like ages, I finally got my horse to slow down and headed back to Bob. He looked us up and down, (picture me gasping and grateful to be alive), checked my horse out, and his comment was: "Well, I shouldn't imagine you will have any time faults!" Really, Robert? Thanks so much!

I was very lucky to be one of Mr. Hutton's students and his riding, training, and life lessons will always be a part of me.

Learning from the Masters

Books are great if you already know how to ride.

A LL HORSE ADDICTS KNOW THERE IS TRUTH in the old saying: "It takes two lifetimes to learn how to ride." We take lessons, attend clinics, and seek education anywhere we can. Like me, you have probably worked hard to apply all this learning to your own riding. If a respected and experienced rider or trainer came to my area, I would be there. French, German, British, and American—they all had their own way of training and their own beliefs. The instruction was always about the horse and what he *should* do and how he *should* look. Usually, I found myself struggling to do what was being asked and not knowing how. It is no surprise that all of the different approaches were confusing! Which way was correct?

Then, of course, there are the books. I read everything I could—all of the classics and endless detailed books about training the horse. They all had plenty of theory and lecture about training horses. (Yes, I *know* my horse is supposed to be 'on the bit,' and 'tracking up' and 'forward,' etc.) What I really needed was clear direction as to *how* we were supposed to accomplish all this *together*.

We humans have been conditioned to learn through reading and studying in school. But when applied to horses this turns out not to be the whole picture. Riding is a physical, kinesthetic sport. It involves two separate and very different beings attempting to work together. This is why the traditional 'read more/study more' method is not the whole story in riding horses.

Theory *is* important, of course. Riding the classical gymnastic exercises in progression, the aids of communication between horse and rider, are the foundation of good training. Without theory, we are just stumbling along without a clear path or direction, which usually results in very slow progress. This is frustrating for riders and not fair to the horses. What I needed was a balance between theory and practical application. I wanted what we all want with our horses—to dance together effortlessly.

I rode or audited with many excellent coaches and clinicians in those years. Each one would have one or two tips, or a good exercise, that would help with my horse. But those were just moments of success, while the big picture seemed to elude me. Then one weekend, after years of clinics and lessons, I attended a clinic in Michigan with Chuck Grant. Chuck was often called 'The Father of American Dressage,' and he was the first rider and trainer to bring quality European masters to the United States. His methods were simple, classical, and positive, and were a wonderful change from the micro-managed, forceful training of others I had seen. He was a master of *less is more* when working with his horses. (I would hear the 'doing less to get more' theory again, regarding the rider, when I met Sally Swift years later.)

One of Chuck's memorable comments was: "Books are great if you already know how to ride." Imagine my relief!

Watching Chuck train was pure pleasure. All of his horses went with happy ears, softly swinging tails, quiet mouths, and obvious enjoyment. No forcing, no punishment, and no drilling. He would ask his horse for a movement, accept what the horse gave him without judgment and ride on, always rewarding every try.

"Ask often, expect nothing, reward frequently," he would say. Chuck let his horses find their own balance and never forced them into a frame, simply letting time and the classic exercises do the job. He had a beautifully quiet seat and position in the saddle, and you rarely saw him give an aid. Chuck *allowed* his horse to carry him every step. As a result, he trained more horses to Grand Prix level than any rider in the country at that time. In addition, Chuck's horses lived long happy lives, were always willing, and stayed sound.

Chuck was a beautiful example of correct, old school classical dressage—happy, relaxed horses in natural self carriage with their heads slightly in front of the vertical, on a soft rein, with amazing lift and balance. This was the type of riding and training I had been looking for. Now I had a visual of my dream, but it was many years before Sally Swift would come on the scene and show me *how* to ride in this way.

Seeking Connection

It is our job, as riders, to be conscious
of what we do in the saddle.

RIDING IN COMPETITIONS HAD ITS OWN REWARDS. It was the icing on the cake when I had a winning jumping round or a good dressage test. But what I really loved was the training— building a connection with my horses and facing challenges together. There is nothing like riding a smooth jump course in total harmony with a horse; finding a rhythmic gallop on cross country and flying over big obstacles without losing a beat. Later on, I would get the same thrill on a good cutting horse or from an effortless dressage ride. I was also given wonderful chances to ride great barrel racing horses, drive draft teams, move cattle on a ranch, and hunt with a hound pack in Michigan. The style of riding doesn't matter. The thrill is about the teamwork with a good horse.

It was obvious to me that teamwork meant *two* of us. Since playing the 'riding game' was my idea I felt that, as a rider, it was my responsibility to work on *myself* in order to be a good team member. The years of riding the jumpers gave me experience with a huge variety of horses. I rode not only my own mounts, but plenty of horses owned by my coaches too. In short, I had sat on enough horses to know that the most important part of the team was *me*.

So when it came to finding a teacher, I wanted my riding instruction to be about helping me improve my own riding skills. I started to avoid the type of teachers who told students to do forceful things to the horse. "Drive him forward! Get him on the bit! Make him bend!" This did not seem logical or fair to me. My job is to learn my horse's language first, so he can understand what I am asking. I wanted to know how I could *help* my horse, not *tell* him.

Very little instruction in those days was about the rider. Also, this was many years before natural horsemanship and ground training became popular. We just got on the horse and tried over and over, hoping for better results. My horses and I had our successes, but I knew that something was missing. I could see the magic in the really great riders I admired, and wanted that magic for myself. At times, I could feel an effortless connection to my horse, but I did not know how it had happened. Those occasional glimpses of being a better *me* on my horses were tantalizing and wonderful. All riders have felt those 'aha' moments on a horse. Looking for that connection is what keeps us riding and learning.

Meeting Sally Swift

Pay more attention to yourself,
with less focus on your horse. — Sally Swift

O NE DAY, IN 1986, A FRIEND CALLED and invited me to attend a clinic with "a little old lady from Vermont" who was supposed to be "quite a kick." That was my introduction to Sally Swift and *Centered Riding*®, and it opened up a whole new world of riding for me. I think of Sally as the true 'Yoda' of teaching. She was the very first instructor who was teaching the *rider* what to do on a horse. Until Sally, traditional instruction focused mainly on the horse, and most riders did not have a clue as to how their bodies were actually affecting their horses. Sally defied conventional teaching by suggesting we pay more attention to ourselves and less to our horses. She taught us how to be aware of and use our *own* bodies, on and off the horse, and to realize how much we really influence our horses.

As Sally worked with students in the lessons, I saw the horses respond to their 'new' riders with beautiful, effortlessly flowing movements. With her simple basics, Sally was able to get riders to relax, release, and allow. They were doing less and accomplishing more. Rider and horse teams were actually enjoying themselves! Sally's unique and fun way of getting through to her students was a real gift, and I became an immediate fan.

Sally Swift. Photo credit Wendy Murdoch.

These were revolutionary concepts at that time and the lessons Sally taught about body awareness for riders were life changing. The days of gripping knees, jammed down heels, and cast iron legs were over. Many pieces of the 'perfect partnership' puzzle were answered by Sally and mirrored back to me by my grateful horses.

It was a humbling time for me and my learning journey totally shifted at that point. I stopped going to competitions so I could study more with Sally. I spent hundreds of saddle hours practicing her methods. I learned to find my center, let go, breathe, and allow. I began to feel the horse's movement under my seat, and learned to follow that movement with my body. Every clinic with Sally brought more awareness. For the next 12-plus years I chased her all over the Midwest and East coast, soaking up her teachings. I was very lucky to spend so much time with her in those years and I am forever grateful.

As I continued to learn from Sally, I began to remember how it felt to ride as a kid again. The fun and joy came back into my riding and the longed for, effortless connection to my horses was happening. *Centered Riding*® was a way to get back to my natural seat and feel on a horse. It was wonderful to find that place again! My horses mirrored every change and release in my body, and responded by giving me relaxed, effortless rides. Thank you Sally, for everything you taught me. It was about so much more than horses, and I live your lessons every day.

Sally Swift on *Doushka*. Photo courtesy of Trafalgar Square Books.

A Lesson with Sally

Breathe, center and grow.

"NOW KAREN, YOU LIKE TO LEAD WITH YOUR CHIN, don't you?" Sally never missed a thing and her brisk New England voice could project effortlessly across any arena. Her timing was always spot-on and she could give you the smallest corrections and make a huge difference in your ride. These adjustments were always about the riders and never about the horses. At Sally's clinics, we would begin each day with two hours of body awareness exercises without the horses, then ride in groups while she talked us through the *Centered Riding*® basics with incredible patience. I never felt pressured in her lessons since she was always positive and supportive. Her simple delight in teaching was something special and she brought us all along on her fun journey. Lessons with Sally always ended on a happy note, with excited riders sharing their discoveries. She changed my way of riding forever.

Sally herself was from the East coast and the hunter world, so she was adept at helping tight and gripping jumper riders like myself. She showed me how to find my center, release my joints, and let go of old habits. The results were beyond what I could have imagined. By correcting simple, basic body issues, I was able to line myself up over my horse's center of gravity and ride with ease, which allowed him to move freely and in natural balance. The longed for effortless connection with my horse was becoming a reality!

A typical group lesson would begin with Sally talking to us about breathing while we warmed up at a walk. "Imagine a bellows in your center, and open and close it with your breath," she would say. "Now picture your legs as hollow breathing tubes and fill them with air. Feel your entire rib cage expand outward as you breathe." Not one of my past teachers had ever mentioned breathing! In fact, I was so good at *not* breathing, that I wasn't even aware there were other options.

Once Sally got us all breathing, she would talk us through her 'walk and the following seat' exercise. She had us simply letting go, walking on a long rein, feet hanging out of the stirrups, and allowing our bodies to feel every movement of the horse. "Breathe into your center. Now feel the alternate lift and drop of your horse's back. Feel your horse's rib cage swinging side to side and allow your legs to follow that motion. Receive the motion of your horse and allow it to move up your spine, releasing it out the top of your head." The result is an easy warm-up for the horse and a total connection between horse and rider—no stress involved!

Her simple concepts and excellent images made all the difference in my riding. It was almost too easy! After some help in balancing each rider in their saddle, she would send us out again to feel the changes and the new connection to our horses. We would move on to posting trot—"Release your hips as you sit in the saddle, and allow your knees to go forward." Transitions were suddenly effortless when Sally would suggest we "center and grow three times before every transition. Use your exhale breath as you allow your body to move into the next gait."

I loved the relaxed pattern of Sally's lessons. It was a wonderful change from the old days of stress, drilling, and often, frustration. Sally would have us all laughing, discovering, and sharing. Her lessons were about experimenting and observing, not forcing and demanding of either rider or horse. She never addressed a horse's 'issues', and we could all see the positive changes happening in the horses as she worked with the riders. Any problems I was having with my horse would disappear when Sally corrected my body. Her methods were completely new concepts at the time, and something that all *Centered Riding*® teachers are now well known for.

Teaching

Have the courage to teach the basics. – Sally Swift

At every *Centered Riding*® clinic, I watched Sally's methods turn struggling students into balanced, effortless-looking riders. I saw happy horses moving beautifully without force or stress. With Sally's help, horses and riders were coming together in harmony and partnership. Watching these miracles happen I would think to myself, *every rider needs to learn this!* Her methods were changing my entire life for the better, not to mention my riding. Just being around Sally, absorbing her balanced, centered energy and her way of looking at the world with lightness and joy, kept her students coming back for more.

So that is how I found myself, after several years of working with Sally, signing up for a *Centered Riding*® instructor course. In 1989 I flew to Wisconsin for the intensive two-part training. My initial intentions were not to teach full time, but to my surprise, helping students and horses turned into a much-loved passion. Thirty years later I cannot imagine a better way to spend my life.

The instructor course included bodywork and awareness sessions, lessons with Sally herself, and 'practice teaching' on our student riders while Sally observed. This unique clinic format actually taught us *how* to teach, definitely a first in those days. *Centered Riding®* courses are still run this way because it is so successful. This is similar to the classical European riding schools, which are set up so the masters train the horses, the students learn from the masters, and the horse mirrors and teaches the student. The student eventually becomes the trainer and their students continue the cycle. In other words, the horse, the rider, and the instructor are all students of each other.

Sally was a great role model for new instructors. She taught us to watch a student with *soft eyes* and to *see the whole* during a lesson. She constantly reminded us that *less is more* in teaching, and to *leave spaces* so that our students have time to feel and process. Her emphasis on the positive word and her ability to make learning fun were a huge influence on me. Lessons with Sally were about sharing, discovering together, and finding the joy in riding.

As for our horses, watching them respond so positively to this style of riding was a real eye opener. There was no *training*, in the traditional sense, done at Sally's clinics. She shared the simple 'Four Basics' that she repeated to us over and over, in many different ways, using wonderful images. She had riders doing less and getting so much more. If you love horses, you cannot help being touched by this much kinder approach to riding.

When I think back to the early days of yelling instructors, frustration, and even tears, I feel so much gratitude to Sally for showing us a more positive way of learning and riding. Students often say to me, "You are the first instructor who has helped *me*, instead of telling me to do something to my horse." That pretty much sums up Sally's unique approach to riding and teaching.

Riding and Life

*Riders who work on themselves OFF the horse, will
improve the most ON the horse. — Sally Swift*

SALLY SWIFT DEVELOPED *Centered Riding*® through her work
with the Alexander Technique, the Feldenkrais Method,
and Tai Chi. These are all bodywork modalities that bring
awareness to our own *use of self.* The premise being, if we are
using our bodies incorrectly, then we are unbalanced, which
causes tension in our muscles. An out-of-balance person
will also work much too hard to accomplish simple, daily
tasks (i.e., walking, running, lifting), not to mention riding!
Our daily habits become our pattern, and over time, incorrect body use leads to chronic pain and possibly injury. Our
horses will reflect our patterns, eventually leading to their
own soundness and pain issues.

This was eye opening information for me. Sally taught us
that to improve our riding, we needed to learn how to use
ourselves correctly *off* the horse. I began to realize that few
of us are connected to our *own* bodies, making it impossible
to truly connect with our horse's body when we ride. The idea
that my own habits and crooked patterns were affecting how
my horses moved, and their health, was all the incentive that
I needed to change.

When we climb onto a horse's back, we are no
longer just a two-legged being, responsible
only for ourselves. Immediately, we affect
another being—our horse.
WE are the direct cause of our horse's ability
to be balanced or not balanced, comfortable
or not comfortable, able to perform or not
able. It is OUR job to be conscious
of what we do in the saddle. – KI

Once you start down the road to better body awareness there is no going back!

I listened seriously to Sally's advice. This led me to weekly Alexander lessons for several years, plus countless workshops since. Tai Chi classes followed, where I learned to center myself and move with flow and rhythm. I found Feldenkrais teachers and learned *awareness through movement.* Later on, deep tissue bodywork would bring even bigger improvements to my riding and my health. There is a payoff in working on oneself that goes way beyond riding. If you have been in pain, then body awareness work can be a way to heal. The natural balance and freedom of movement that we can all have, at any age, is well worth the time spent in study. This wonderful ease of movement has a huge impact in my daily life, in everything I do, from peeling carrots to pushing wheelbarrows.

The horses I rode loved all of the changes I was making. Focusing on myself took the pressure off the horse and they were more than willing to meet me half way. As I became more balanced and free moving, they naturally came into balance under me. Riding well means more than being physically fit. It is also about self-awareness, humility and a positive attitude. This means continual study of ourselves as balanced human beings so we can be fair and responsible partners for our horses.

Sally walked her talk in this aspect. She was born with a serious scoliosis and the doctors in that day said she was headed toward a wheel chair for life. Instead, because of her bodywork study and practice, Sally rode horses, jumped, hunted, and led a very active life. As her student, I was in awe of her accomplishments in the face of such challenges. She was a master who lived her teachings and she made believers of all her students simply because of who she was. Sally changed so many of us forever and influenced riding teachers all over the world. At this writing there are about 400 certified *Centered Riding®* instructors in the USA and more than 500 in Europe. Her original book has been published in 17 languages and can be found in the libraries of top riding schools. To be a part of the legacy that Sally left us riders and teachers has been a life changing and priceless gift.

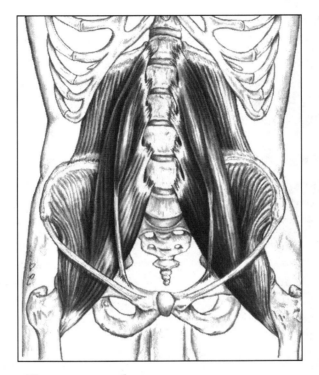

The psoas muscles. Drawing courtesy of Robin Dorn.

Core Truths

Learning to ride from the inside out.

HOW OFTEN, IN A LESSON, HAVE YOU BEEN TOLD to "use your core" and "tighten your abs," while riding? Did this make you feel tense? Was your horse stiff and resisting? Did you try harder, thinking you would never be strong enough? In the dressage world, especially, our core muscles are usually described as the *outside* mid-section muscles: the abdominals, obliques, etc. We are told to use these muscles around our middle by strengthening and holding them. I knew from previously trying to forcefully use my abs that this only created a stiff, bouncing me in the saddle and a very unhappy horse. It was definitely not fun for either one of us! My history with Sally had shown me that a tight mid-section just locked up my entire body. At this point in my riding—going from the initial years of tightness and tension, to learning to let go through *Centered Riding®* methods—I knew there had to be a happy medium between the two styles. I could see this effortless looking balance when watching the really great riders. But again, how did they get there?

So the question is—how to be stable in the saddle without being too tight or too loose? How can I flow with my horse's movements, have a secure seat and independent aids, all at the same time?

As usual, when a student is ready—along comes our next teacher, right? While I was at this in-between period in my riding life, a friend brought me a copy of the book *Zen and Horseback Riding* by Tom Nagel. She had seen Tom give a talk at the Midwest Horse Fair in Wisconsin about the use of our ***psoas muscles*** in riding. Tom had also written about the concepts of posture, breath, and awareness—which were very compatible with my *Centered Riding*® training. But the real *aha* moment in his book, for me, was the detailed biomechanical information about the human body as it applies to riding a horse. Tom was the first instructor I had heard of who was describing the psoas muscles specifically as the *true core* of the body.

Tom's ideas were intriguing and I wanted to learn more, so in 2005 my friend Sue Ennis and I invited him to teach a clinic in Michigan. That weekend, Tom taught us how to access our psoas muscles through simple exercises and demonstrations. We learned how to balance, move, and ride with true stability just by becoming aware of our psoas. For me, the results were dramatic. When I rode my horse in the afternoon sessions, it felt like I was super-glued to his back at every step and able to follow his movement in all gaits, from collected to extended. Because of my new core stability, my horse responded by using his own 'core' (yes, horses have psoas muscles, too), and he was able to give me even more lift and collection than I had ever felt before. We were effortlessly moving together, every step, in perfect harmony. It was definitely a light-bulb moment!

How and why does this dramatic change happen? Simply because we are using our bodies in the way they were designed. Tom explains this as "riding from the inside out" versus "riding from the outside in." Classically, most instructors will talk about using our *outside* muscles when we ride, which results in forceful methods and tension. We have all tried this at some point! This tension translates directly to our horses and restricts their movement. When we ride from the inside out, using our true core/psoas, we become stable in the saddle. This inside stability allows freedom of our outside muscles, and this freedom of movement will immediately have the same effect on our horses.

I sent the following email to Tom after his clinic:

Tom, I believe that what you are teaching is truly the key to the dream that all riders aspire to—being one with our horses. In 20-plus years of riding, I have never been to such a place! My friend Sue and I rode our horses again right after your clinic. We had a blast applying our new psoas awareness to shoulder in, leg yields, haunches in, half-passes, transitions, etc. It was incredible and easy, and we were both laughing with the joy of it all. My horse was happily moving around the arena in effortless self-carriage and willing to do whatever I asked! We were completely connected, in mind and body. Thank you for coming to Michigan and sharing your teachings with us.

Without getting too technical I want to share my version of 'Psoas 101' with you, so bear with me! Here goes:

The psoas are the only muscles that connect our upper and lower body. Without them we could not walk, stand, run, or pursue any sport. They are our *invisible core,* so deep in the body that very few of us are aware of them. Out of sight, out of mind, as the saying goes. Why is this major muscle group so important for riding? Nearly everything our instructors are asking us to do initiates with using our psoas. When you balance your pelvis vertically in the saddle (neither arched or collapsed), your psoas muscles are able to lengthen and fall back in the pelvis. This will give you immediate stability in the saddle. Because of this inner stability, your lower back will lengthen and relax, and your hip joints will release and open. Releasing the hips allows your legs to lengthen and drop. This gives you that wonderfully secure 'wrapped around your horse' feeling, without pinching or gripping. (And that long leg that the dressage riders desire!) In addition, because we have a pair of psoas muscles, one on each side of our spine, we have a wide variation of motion—so we can match our horse's movements in each gait, through transitions, lateral work, etc., without blocking him. This is the way to riding in correct, classical seat.

This discovery was the missing piece that I needed, and it completely changed my riding. I was now able to sit the extended trot and ride an effortless canter. My legs magically dropped and all of my joints were flexible. I felt lifted, lengthened, and completely solid within all of my horse's movements. Transitions were easy and fluid. Everyone can do this if they have the knowledge and are willing to practice the exercises. The concepts are simple and they work. The exercises are easy. The payoff is huge!

From my journal:

Riding with Sally's Centered Riding techniques, added to the psoas lessons from Tom, it feels like the puzzle pieces are really fitting together. I am able to ride with the same strength and tone that I had in my jumping days, but now I am supple and flexible too. The combination is amazing and powerful, not only on the horses, but in everyday life. In riding, my horses are more confident and relaxed. They love having a secure rider, yet they also appreciate the flexibility within the strength so they can move freely. Whether it's a half pass, a jump, or a gallop on the trail, I am stable in the saddle, yet able to allow my horses to move in their own balance. In daily life, I move with better posture and awareness, and more confidence and ease in all situations. Old pain from incorrect posture and way of moving is gone. This has brought me back to a place in my riding body and strength that I remember, but with the distinct difference of being able to flow and connect with my horse in every movement. It is magical!

Combining my early coaching in classical technique and theory with both Sally's and Tom's methods has given me a more complete picture of what good riding is about. Clearly, unless we are one of the rare and gifted riders, we average mortals *do* need specific information on *how* to physically use our bodies on (and off) a horse. Otherwise we struggle along, making slow progress, hoping for a magic wand to make us into a great rider one day. So I highly encourage you all to read Tom's book, *Zen and Horseback Riding*, and *Centered Riding* by Sally Swift for more detailed information on their methods.

Humans are Vertical, Horses are Horizontal

Riding is an optical illusion.

D URING A LESSON ONE DAY, with yet another student who had previously been taught to 'drive with her seat'—it was suddenly obvious to me what was really going on. As I watched the horse and rider I saw a *horizontally moving horse* carrying a *designed to function vertically* human rider. This sounds obvious, but it was a huge *aha* at that moment. The vertical and horizontal difference between horse and human became very clear. The rider, like so many of us, believed that she was supposed to push with her seat to go with her horse. (I often jokingly call this 'scooter butt'.) Pushing is a horizontal movement. This front-to-back motion of the rider's seat only results in interference with the horse's back, and his ability to move forward freely.

In reality, there is no such thing as a 'driving seat'. Think about the riders you have seen who are busily pushing and shoving on poor *Dobbin's* back. All because they have been told to do so. Usually *Dobbin* has his ears pinned back, tail swishing, a hollow back, and shortened movement. He is not being naughty or lazy, he is trying to tell his rider that pushing on the saddle is painful for him. A horse cannot connect from back to front when a rider with a busy seat is blocking his movement. Eventually he ends up with a sore back, stifled gaits, and lameness issues.

In this light bulb moment during the lesson, I asked the student to *remain vertical*, stop pushing with her seat, and *allow* the motion from her horse to travel *vertically up and down* her body, instead of front to back. This simple direction made obvious sense to the rider and she was able to quietly *receive* her horse's movement and let it move vertically up and out the top of her head. The change in her horse when she did this was amazing. He began to relax and round his back, lengthen his stride, and reach out to the bit. They floated around the arena together, totally connected, light and happy.

Humans are Vertical. We balance and move as vertical beings.
Drawing by Barbara Clark.

When I explained this concept to Tom Nagel he replied, "So riding is actually an optical illusion." When you watch a horse and rider, it looks like the rider is moving her horse forward, but in reality she simply remains vertical and *allows* her horse to *carry* her forward. This concept reminds me of the theory of *receive and let flow,* which is the basis of Tai Chi and all martial arts. This is exactly what good riders are doing in the saddle.

We, as humans, are *vertical beings.* We move and balance as upright, two-legged creatures. When we get on a horse, we are *still* vertical beings. If we do not "honor our verticality," as my Alexander Technique teacher says, then we are off balance, carrying tension, and not stable. When you observe people who move with good balance and body awareness, notice that they appear vertical in all that they do. Think of the great dancers, gymnasts, and skilled athletes that you have seen. They look smooth, fluid, and effortless in their movements. This is because they know how to use their bodies effectively, from their core, with full extension. As riders, we need to remember that we are vertical beings while we ride. This is essential for our own true balance and our horse's comfort.

Horses are Horizontal.
They balance and move as horizontal beings.
Drawing by Barbara Clark.

In contrast, horses are *horizontal beings.* They move as four-legged, horizontal creatures. Their energy flows horizontally through their bodies. They move like horses, not humans! So, to match human and horse together, we need to balance our vertical selves over our horizontal horses. Meaning: our own center should line up over our horse's center. Our center is low in our pelvis and the horse's center is located just behind his shoulders. When these two centers are in alignment and the rider is vertical, it allows our horse to move like a horse. And he will be able to do this with freedom and natural self-carriage.

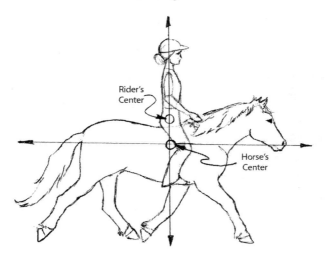

The horse carries the rider forward.
Drawing by Barbara Clark.

This simple awareness really influenced my own riding and teaching. You can experiment with this movement yourself. First, find your quiet vertical balance and simply *allow* your horse to carry you forward. Focus on not using your seat to get your horse to move! (Note: At first, your horse may not understand the change in you and he might go slower. Resist the urge to push and kick. You might need a crop to gently wake your horse up to your new, quiet self. Some riders have taught their horse to tune them out by working too hard with their bodies.)

Once your horse's energy is really working, you will feel his movement travel up through your body, lifting and dropping your seat, alternately left and right. As you get used to this lift and drop you can feel your own back and hips release. Each left and right lift in your seat will begin to travel *diagonally* across your upper body. This is true, natural bilateral movement. It is the same diagonal movement we have when we are walking with a relaxed torso and swinging arms. Your horse's strides will lengthen and his back will release and lift. This is how you build correct forward energy in your horse. Just receive, allow and think vertically!

Karen with *Andy*.

Andy

ANDY IS MY CURRENT RIDING PARTNER AND TEACHER. He is a Haflinger gelding who was born in Michigan. I met him when he was four years old and was instantly smitten. *Andy* has an amazing, happy go lucky attitude and he is willing to play any game that I suggest with pleasure. His daily greeting is always: "Hi! What are we going to do today?" He is up for anything, dressage, jumping, trail riding, obstacle games, and especially the beach. He is sound, sane, and always a gentleman. As a young rider, I never had a pony because I went right into show hunters. So, in middle age, to find such a fun, willing, and happy pony partner is like going back to my kid years to live out a dream.

We are fortunate if we get one horse in our lifetime that is that special partner. Lucky me, I have had several horses who took me on some wonderful journeys in competition and learning, and to have this amazing friend in my post-competition days has been a real gift. I found *Andy* while I was traveling and teaching full time around the country and was between horses. His steady mind, grounded self, and honest attitude were exactly what I needed. He made my hectic travel life possible because he was always the same sweet, generous guy when I came home, even after weeks of being away.

Andy gives my ever-changing life balance and a feeling of 'coming home.' When I need a lesson, he gives me exactly the right one. When I need a grounded, calm friend to just hang out with and let go of stress, he is always there for me.

He also has a wonderful sense of humor! If I am being too serious and caught up in life's details, he will bring out his silly self to make me laugh and find my sense of fun and play.

I was very lucky to find him and have him in my life. Thanks buddy, you rock!

Movement

Swimming with sea turtles.

YEARS AGO, ON A SAILING TRIP in the Virgin Islands, I had the amazing opportunity to swim with several giant sea turtles. It was a life changing experience that I will always remember. The turtles were stately, calm, and so graceful for their size. I was wearing snorkel gear and I floated along, watching them with respect for their space, and stayed very quiet. The turtles saw me, but let me join them and swim beside them. I found myself copying the movement of their flippers with my own arms. They made slow, smooth figure eights with their front flippers, which was mesmerizing. I floated alongside them, making figure eights with my own arms, and feeling very calm and fluid.

Sea Turtle. Drawing by Barbara Clark.

I took that incredible feeling of stately peace home with me and into my daily life. I soon discovered that the figure eight of energy was happening in all areas of my body, not just my arms. I also felt this movement in my head and neck, hips, ankles, and spine. This awareness affected everything I did and brought incredible fluidity and ease to daily tasks.

One day, after the sea turtle adventure, I was riding *Andy* and a light bulb went on. I realized that *his* energy was also moving through his entire body in a continuous figure eight direction! The change of awareness in my own body had allowed *Andy* to release and move in his own figure eight of energy. The only difference between us is that my energy

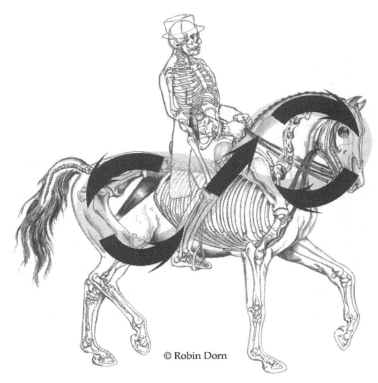

© Robin Dorn

Image courtesy of Robin Dorn.

moves in a *vertical* figure eight, and his energy moves in a *horizontal* figure eight. As I balanced over his center of gravity, just behind his shoulders, I immediately felt that the cross point of our *eights* was connected. Our energies flowed together and I had one of the best rides of my life that day. It was amazing—fluid and effortless, with a calm, continuous recycling power. At that moment on *Andy's* back, I remembered the sea turtles and realized that *all* beings move in the same way, with a figure eight shaped, steady flow.

© Robin Dorn

Image courtesy of Robin Dorn.

From my journal:

Today, while riding Andy, I discovered the secret of the flowing cycle of energy in my body and my horses' body. I was warming up, breathing and relaxing into Andy's lovely swinging back and allowing him to move my body. It can become a meditation on a horse with a supple body, and I was totally mesmerized with the feeling. I was really 'in the flow' with my breath and movement as Andy carried me along and it reminded me of my sea turtle adventure. Suddenly I felt something that I had not been aware of before – this incredible figure eight of movement in Andy's body, from the inside out! He would engage his hind end to bring a back leg forward; I felt the flow of that energy come up to his center. Then that flow continued up and over his neck and around his poll and back to my hands. It kept moving in this very natural figure eight pattern that I knew in that moment is the key to how all beings move. It was an effortless, continuous flow of recycling energy. I felt my own body copying his movement. It was like the tide ebbing in and out and my breathing matched the flow. We were moving together, with no effort other than being in the moment of it. His strides got very lofty, light and suspended. The world around us disappeared and we were in our own timeless bubble. For a very practical person like myself, this sounds a bit crazy! But this experience changed my riding times from focused practice to simply allowing and being. With no effort at all, I had an amazing, connected ride with my horse. It is another huge discovery piece, and has evolved into much more than riding. Being aware of this continuous, flowing 'eight' is how we can move through life with ease in every moment.

In the drawing you can see where the two figure eights align, with one center above the other. The rider's figure eight is vertical and the horse's figure eight is horizontal. This figure-eight path of energy travels on the *inside* of both horse and human bodies. If you are aware of these paths of energy in you and your horse, and how they relate, you can find an amazing connection in every step!

Riding the Crest of the Wave

Surfing, sailing and riding.

From my journal:

Today I had a beautiful morning's sail on my little Sunfish boat. The winds were high and it was an exhilarating ride on the lake! Sailing back to the beach, I was running before the wind on large, cresting waves. A wave would pick up my little boat; we would fly along the crest and whoosh down again. Another wave, up we went, surfing along the crest, and whoosh! It was the infinite, recycling energy of the water, and it was nature at its best. You either go along for the ride, or you capsize!

(Happy to write that I loved every minute, and made it back to the beach!)

That same afternoon, I went out to ride my horse, with the sense of the waves still in my body and awareness. Because of the winds and the energy in the air, my horse was really 'up' and giving me a very forward ride. I was still in sailing mode and I unconsciously let myself ride the wave of his super energy and enjoy it. If you are going to get on, then ride it and go with it! So around the arena we went, with me feeling his energy come up under me and 'crest' in front of my seat. I let him lift me, balanced on the crest as he carried us forward, and whooshed down, over and over. It was fabulous!

My horse was elastic, suspended, and lifting like I had not felt before. We actually achieved a truly amazing passage and collected trot. And I realize now, while I write, that we were in perfect self-carriage together. In the past I would have tried to control his fabulous energy and blocked it. But today, I went with it, allowed it to move through me, helped him rebalance it, and ended up with one fancy pony ride!

"Riding the Waves." Drawing by Barbara Clark.

Breath is Life

Breathe—you are alive! – Tich Naht Hahn

ONE OF MY STUDENTS HAD A VERY CLEVER HORSE. His name was *Bumpkin* and he had his own ways of telling his rider when she was not behaving as a good rider should. He was a fantastic teacher and his methods of communicating with his owner and me during our lessons would have us laughing hysterically. But we also learned more from *Bumpkin* than any books or master trainers could have taught us. Mostly we learned to *listen!* When *Bumpkin* felt Sue, his rider, getting off balance, he would wiggle around for a few steps, then bring her right to me in the middle of the arena, plant his feet, obviously saying: "Fix her now!" If her legs were gripping too tightly, he would move like a tiny pony with little short steps. If she looked down instead of focusing outward, he would stop immediately. He was a master teacher and a perfect mirror for his rider.

One day, in a lesson, he began to breathe very strangely, taking huge breaths with his rib cage moving in and out in a very exaggerated way. We were concerned and thought that he was having some terrible issue with his health. (He was not a young horse at the time.) Sue brought him down to a walk and as I watched them, I realized that *she* was breathing very shallowly and with restricted movement in her own rib cage. I said to her, "*Bumpkin* is telling you to breathe!" We both laughed, but got the point. Sue began to breathe fully, and *Bumpkin* happily trotted along again with calm breathing and a relaxed rib cage. He had once again given us silly humans another good lesson.

To ride with our breath
is the ultimate simplicity.

I have been taught many different ways to breathe over the years. There are dozens of opinions about correct breathing—from yoga instructors, physical therapists, and more. It was all very confusing! I learned about our breathing diaphragm, when to inhale, when to exhale, belly breathing, counting while breathing, you name it I tried it. What frustrated me the most was that I had to *think* too much about this seemingly simple and natural action.

Finally, I learned to quit working at it and simply let my breathing happen. As I inhale quietly and slowly, I can feel my body expand and lengthen upward and downward simultaneously from my center. My entire rib cage expands naturally. The exhale is a slow, effortless release of air upward and out my mouth. I feel my lower back release and my seat relax into the saddle. In other words: *I allow my body to breathe itself.* This is the way that bodies *like* to breathe.

A simple way to become aware of your breathing is to lie on the floor with knees bent and allow your breath to flow in and out quietly. Feel the connection of your back to the ground and your whole body release and relax as you breathe. Avoid over doing and over thinking. Let the flow of your breath happen naturally. The change of inhale to exhale should be seamless. I used to work much too hard at exhaling, then I would have to take a huge gulp of air inward. It was exhausting! And I could not keep it up for long!

How does our breathing affect our horse? When horses are afraid, their bodies tense up and they hold their breath. When a rider stops breathing fully, our eyes become tense and hard focused, and our entire body becomes stiff. We don't intend it, but this tension is warning our horse to be afraid. At the beginning of lessons I will ask my students to just simply breathe and forget everything else. Shut down our 'busy mind' and just simply, *breathe*. It is the very best thing you can do for your horse, yourself and the connection between the two of you. Many, many times, I have watched a ready to explode horse be calmed by a rider who begins to breathe consciously.

You can practice off your horse by taking this simple, natural breathing into your day—while washing dishes, walking the dog, sitting at your desk, speaking to a group. You may find yourself using less effort to do simple tasks and a wonderful sense of calm and peace. This awareness of how we breathe is very important when we are around other beings—both two and four legged. Peaceful, calm breathing can create good relationships.

These days, I have no conscious thought of breathing at all. The effortless, flowing breath has become a part of me. I appreciate my ability to breathe every morning, every day, and throughout the day. I know my horse appreciates the way I breathe because he does the same, along with me. If I forget for a moment, I think of *Bumpkin* again, and his hilarious style of teaching!

And I breathe

The Art of Listening

Lessons from the master pony.

From my journal:

Finally! Good weather and the freedom for actual saddle time with Andy yesterday! I left my phone and the dogs in the house and escaped to the barn. In classic Andy style, he delivered the exact lesson and ride that I needed for that day. Inside that cute fuzzy pony is quite an intuitive being, and I have learned in my 'wiser' years that it is good for me to listen and go along with his plan. He knows more that I ever will about life and taking in the moments. Music is on in the area. I am saddled up, mounted up, and since it had been a week since my last ride, I was carefully warming him up. We are stretching, riding on bending lines for suppleness, and basic lateral work, all at the walk. Andy was very soft and felt great. When I halted to do some collecting back up steps, Andy suddenly got stiff, head up and resisting. I took a minute, gave him a couple of pats, and tried another back up. Not happening! Andy told me very clearly, "Enough of this! Let's just DO it!" Next thing I know, he has collected his whole body up like a mini grand prix horse, arched his neck and taken us into a fantastic collected trot, back swinging and soft as butter. I giggled and smiled—and off we went, around the arena doing his favorite show off moves: haunches in, half pass, etc. We took a little break, trotted off again, and I 'thought' about half steps and a more animated trot—and he immediately offered a VERY elevated trot, with the pauses between steps that are the start of a real passage! I basically did nothing but think it and let my body follow him.

More amazing lessons from the Master Pony: Be in the moment, listen, honor your partner at all times, and enjoy the ride! (And by the way, when Andy offered his passage steps, the music playing was "Dancing Cheek to Cheek." All that and he has a great sense of humor too!)

When I was younger and working hard at training it seemed important to follow the correct steps of gymnastic schooling. I believed, with my human ego, that I knew more than my horses did about proper development. Years later I have come to realize that simply listening to my horse is my finest skill. He will tell me when he is ready for each new movement, and offer things freely when he is able. After all, it is my *horse* who is actually carrying *me*, and not the other way around! The real 'dance' with my horses did not happen until I was mature enough to realize this.

If I get on my horse with a listening and open mind, amazing things happen. If I fall back into my old 'end gaining' attitude, it does not go so well! Believe me, our horses know the difference! I remember an observation from one of my old teachers, Chuck Grant. He had been a very successful dressage master who dedicated his life to his horses. He rode well into his eighties and when he was finally unable to ride any longer, he commented: "The hardest part of having to give up riding is that I was *just* starting to get it." Chuck was right. Time has taught me to be mindful, every day and every ride, of my horses' own frame of mind and desires.

The Eyes Have It!

Look up and see the world around you!

I AM WATCHING A GROUP OF STUDENTS *lead their horses at one of my clinics. We are playing with groundwork exercises and patterns, off the horse. The students are practicing their body language, breathing, and balance toward achieving a closer partnership with their horses. I have put some fun, upbeat music on my PA system to help my students 'find the dance' with their horse. But, as I watch the group, every single person is looking down at the ground as they lead their horse. They are thinking so hard and trying so hard that they have lost all sense of awareness of anything around them. (Not to mention what their horse is doing!) The students are leaning forward, out of balance, and breathing poorly. The horses are on their forehand, out of balance, dragging their feet, and looking depressed. It was clear to me that they would probably do the same things in the saddle. In other words:*

We ride like we walk!

In the past, my own teachers would tell me (10 million times per lesson) to "Look Up!" So I would pick my head up, for at least two whole seconds, and then back down I would go. Like one of those crazy bobble-head dolls. Obviously, there is more to looking up than just lifting my head! *The real key is in how we use our eyes.* Most of us spend so much time looking inward, that we have lost awareness of the excellent peripheral vision we have. We humans actually have 180-degree vision. Who knew?! We spend most of our day looking at the ground as we walk, or forcing our head up briefly when we remember. As a rider who used to struggle with this constantly, it was a life change for me to learn from Tom Nagel about 'looking 180-degrees.' A whole new visual world opened up for me, on and off my horse!

When I asked the students at this clinic to simply be aware of their peripheral vision, and their entire surroundings, the changes were incredible. The humans became balanced, softer, and started breathing better. The horses became light, forward and moved with happy attitudes. Everyone was 'dancing' with the music and in true partnership with their horse, all because they simply expanded their vision and awareness.

Horses live in a high state of awareness. They are prey animals and always on the lookout for a predator. Their very survival depends on it. They want a leader who is aware of their surroundings. Horses will trust a rider who is 180-degree aware. Riders who stare at their horse's neck, or at the ground, do not give their horse the confidence and support that is needed. In fact, staring at the neck of a horse with focused, intense eyes is actually threatening to him. A rider can calm a 'spooking' horse just by becoming aware of her peripheral vision.

I like to practice 180-degree awareness throughout my day; while driving the car, doing chores, or teaching a lesson. I love how this changes my view of the world. So put your cellphones away friends! Look around you!

From my journal:

Today I got on my horse with the intention to practice the simple basics of soft eyes and peripheral awareness. If I caught myself looking at his neck, or thinking too much about details, I simply expanded my 'field', and felt instantly balanced and tall in the saddle. With this peripheral awareness, I was totally connected to my horse through my seat. My energy flowed effortlessly and my aids were light and invisible. When I am 180-degree aware, my entire body is balanced and open, and I breathe fully. Every time that I looked down, I was immediately out of balance and lost connection with my horse. I went back to my 'wide angle view,' and we were dancing to the music again!

Letting Go

The lesson of life.

WHEN I FIRST GET ON MY HORSE and we walk out for our warm up, I never have a plan. I simply sit in the saddle and *be*. Be present, be quiet, be patient. My best rides happen when I have no agenda, no goals, and let the ride take its own path. If I begin this way, I always end up with a happy, light, elastic, and responsive horse. If I begin simply, everything becomes possible. I slow myself down and I breathe. By focusing on me, I take the pressure off my sensitive horse. He has time to warm up his large body and connect with me, because I am willing to wait for that connection. It takes as long as it takes, and it is different for every horse and every ride. In our two-legged impatience we often neglect this simple, kind, and fair warm-up of our four-legged friend. As I wait for my horse, my ride for that day develops in its own way. If I am truly listening and patient, my horse will *offer* some amazing movements. And we can go on from there. His offers of lovely bend will turn into more advanced lateral moves. His light, collected trot will turn into more elevated half steps and passage. He gives all this freely, with enjoyment, because I have waited for him.

Dancing with my body above my horse—not pushing; not demanding. Just waiting for my horse to come up and find me. And he does—every time. – KI

Letting go is one of the best life lessons that our horses have to teach us. They live in the present at every moment. In order to connect with them, we have to be present ourselves. And yes, we ALL bring our 'stuff' to the barn and often forget to leave it at the gate. In the past I would show up at the barn with a plan, a goal-driven agenda, and become frustrated when that riding session did not work out the way I had intended. These are 'end-gaining' methods, as Sally Swift would say. The same thing would happen in lessons with my students. On my way to work with a student, I might be thinking—'this rider has been doing so well, I think she is ready to start half pass today.' I get to the student's barn, and find out that she has had a stressful week and no time to ride. So back to the basics we go, breathing and centering, and riding calming exercises at a walk.

At this writing, I am starting a young dog in a beginner agility class with an incredible mentor and teacher. Every dog in the class is at a different level of confidence and skills, and this changes week to week. At each class I watch, fascinated, as our instructor adjusts the exercises to make every dog and their handler successful. No dog is ever pushed and confidence builds at each session. Real teamwork is growing through time and practice. And, best of all, my dog and I are truly having fun, and we leave each class feeling successful and confident. Yet again, less is more. Patience and listening to what our animal friends need *at that moment* is the point.

When you are spending time with your horse (or your dog!) slow down, watch and listen. Leave your expectations at the gate. Ask yourself, 'how can I help my horse be successful today?' Remember, we humans chose this game of riding. It is our job to allow time and space for our partner's success.

From my journal:

*Today I got on a **FRESH** pony that wanted nothing to do with 'formal schooling.' After walking for 20 minutes, his warm up trot was a total, upside-down rushing madness, and he was **NOT** to be told differently! So, I shortened my stirrups, went into a light jumping position above Andy's back, and to his total delight, we galloped around the arena! To help this experience have some kind of purpose, for me at least (and for survival!) I thought about my own position and riding. I dropped into my center, lined my spine up right over Andy's spine, and allowed all that excess energy from him to flow up and out through my body, in rhythm with his movement.*

I felt incredibly balanced and light! Because of my stable center, I could release my leg joints and they flexed easily with Andy's gallop strides, like the shock absorbers on a car. My arms moved forward and back in rhythm with his neck. Every part of us matched each other. The result was, even at speed, Andy was fast but balanced, and our corners upright with correct bend. When I felt myself get a bit ahead of his center, I rebalanced my own center and realigned my spine over Andy's spine, and we were connected. It was a fun and freeing ride for both of us!

*Andy **LOVED** it—and it was a great lesson for me in going with what we have for the day. Forget my agenda and be present. Every day is a new horse. Ride the one you have under you and enjoy it!*

Bruce Sandifer on *Lego*.

Ride the Up

The secret to lift and collection.

R IDERS HAVE HEARD OVER AND OVER that to get collection, their horse must 'track up' and 'move from behind.' So the rider often ends up pushing with their seat and trying to drive their horse forward with exaggerated aids. Their horse resists, pushes back, and gets even heavier in the hands. Typically human, we have made so much work out of something that horses are capable of doing on their own! Every day-old foal can do beautiful collected trot and passage, and perfect lead changes. As a rider, I do not make my horse do these movements. That would be forcing him, which is *not* what I want to do, and it is physically impossible anyway. I simply think of how my own body needs to work so my horse can perform. Then I ask, and then receive the flow of the horse's energy through my own body.

> ***Nothing forced can ever be beautiful.***
> ***– Phythagorus***

So how do we *ride the up* to get effortless collection? I start in my center, tipping the front of my pelvis slightly upward, and release my lower back. This asks my horse to tip his own pelvis and sit more behind. Then, as Carrie tells it so perfectly in her story below, I think of allowing the *up* from behind my sternum, and up the front of my spine. I visualize the energy flowing up and out the top of my head as I exhale. If I want a bit more energy from my horse, then I add very light, rhythmic leg aids as needed. If I feel the urge to demand more with my seat or my muscles, I remind myself that collection begins with me and to not force my horse into it. Instead, I rebalance myself, send my energy up, breathe, and repeat.

A student's story:

'Ride the Up' is one of my new favorite mantras. I have spent many years trying to feel more secure, more fluid, more everything that we think in our minds will help us to ride our horses better. One afternoon, while riding in Karen's Classical Training Group Class, she was discussing with us how to ride every stride. Always before, I thought that meant to follow the horse down and let the horse's movement take me back up. Wow, what a difference a day makes. Karen explained how to ride all phases of the stride, not just following and making the horse do all the work.

To me, 'riding the up' motion of the stride was one of the biggest 'aha' moments of my life! Always before my concentration had been on 'down'. You know— grounding, keeping my seat deep in the saddle, etc.— with everything focused towards the ground. Now, when I think, 'ride the up' in the saddle, my whole body moves better, in rhythm with the horse, and surprise, my seat is practically glued to the saddle! I am more secure, and riding is much easier than it has ever been.

I guess all those years of reaching for the ground has taught me that you get what you reach for. So Ride the Up! You will reach for your horse and he will be eternally grateful. – Carrie B.

The following words were written by Bruce Sandifer, who is a traditional bridle horse trainer from California. I very much admire his kind and patient approach to training his horses, and his emphasis on riding in a way to help them find their own natural balance.

It doesn't take force to create more movement in a horse. It takes better timing and being in a balanced position so that it's the easiest thing for the horse to do, not something he HAS to do because of pressure or force. Pressure and force tend to slow down a movement, and it then requires even more pressure and force to get things to work even half as effectively. – Bruce Sandifer

Karen and *Bar None*.

Clear Intent

We get what we ask for!

BAR NONE, MY EVENT HORSE, *is galloping easily under me as we approach one of the less difficult obstacles on the five-mile cross-country course at Gladstone, New Jersey. It is the second phase at a regional competition and the course is tough. We are about halfway around the course and have already made it over some of the more difficult jumps, so it feels like we have a 'bit of a breather' coming up. My focus wanders for a split second as I suddenly realize that we are in first place after the dressage phase, and with the way my horse is going now, we have a good chance to finish well, even win. In the split second that my focus wanders, so does my intent. The next obstacle is a simple stair-step type jump and my horse decides that if his rider (me) is not going to be on task, then he is not going to make the effort! I am in shock as my usually super honest jumper simply gallops around the side of an easy jump. My horse knew exactly how to tell me to be present! Pay attention! Keep my clear intent!*

Clear intent is the most important way we communicate with our animal partners. More important than any physical aids we use. Since horses are not truly verbal beings, they rely on our intentions and our body language. Intent means our energy force, our confidence, our clarity of thought. Clear intent goes ninety percent of the way toward accomplishing what we want with our horses. If we are unsure, then we are sending mixed and confusing messages to our horse. Remember the story about students leading their horses while looking down? The simple change of looking outward and being clear instantly changed the whole picture of partnership. In other words, we get what we ask for!

Visualization is a powerful tool to help with our clear intent. How many times do we ask our horse for something, without a clear picture in our head of what we want to accomplish? Our four-legged friends are very good at picking up our mental pictures. We all know this. My dogs *know*, even if I have done nothing to get ready, whether they are going to the doggie park to play, or to the vet. Horses are the same. If I ask for a turn, or a halt, or a leg yield, without a clear picture in my head, I am probably not going to get it. Or it will be a sloppy or forced version of what I wanted. If I play a video of a perfect halt or circle in my head, several times *before* I ask my horse to do it, then he is prepared; he *hears* me, and he is ready.

If my intent is clear, and I am listening to my horse, then I can feel when he is ready, and we perform together, with ease and flow.

To be clear we also need to be prepared. In my jumping days, I would walk the cross country and stadium courses three times; once to just see it, the second time to plan my lines between jumps, and the third time to put everything together in my mind. After that, I would sit quietly and 'ride' the whole course in my mind, over and over. I would play a mental video of my perfect ride, close up, in slow motion. I also used this method at dressage shows to remember the

Mia showing clear intent at an agility trial.
Photo courtesy Mary Burlingame.

patterns, and I do the same thing for dog agility. Taking the time for preparation means that I don't have to *think* about where I am going—I know! And my four-legged partner appreciates my clear intent.

Note to self from my journal:

If I am prepared, then I can let go of goals or agenda and breathe myself into my quiet place. This way I will end up in 'the zone' with my partner and things flow almost in slow motion. Best of all—I have truly ENJOYED the journey, the course, each moment, and the time with my partner. Be prepared, then allow and enjoy!

So, going back to the cross country story: After my horse's refusal and my wake up call, I get my act together and 'get clear' in my thoughts as I circle *Bar None* around and back to the jump we missed. Of course he flies over it easily and we finish the rest of the course clean and in good time. And I never lost my focus on a course again. Another great life lesson from my horse!

Monkey Mind

How to stop the chatter.

From my journal:

Today, I was schooling a friend's mare, when something that I had said to a student in a recent lesson popped into my head. This student had been carrying on a non-stop conversation with herself while she was riding her horse, repeating everything I said and adding her own self-critique and negative comments. Because of all this 'chatter,' she had no connection to her horse and was not even aware of it. She was too busy talking and trying to remember everything at once. 'Monkey Mind,' as my Tai Chi instructor calls it, was hard at work in her head!

So I said to her: "When you are too busy talking, you cannot feel your horse." I suggested that she just breathe, get quiet, and let go of her list of instructions. As soon as her chatter stopped, she and her horse found a connection and ended up having a lovely ride together.

On my friend's horse, I suddenly realized that I was stuck in the same busy, over-thinking pattern.

We all do this at times—appointments, work, kids, or the challenges of a particular horse, etc. The horse I was working with was an Appaloosa mare named Trucker, who is very sensitive and reactive. She is the kind of horse that can trick a rider into exaggerated aids, over-correcting, and always anticipating her next 'spook.' I was far too busy 'training' Trucker to have any real connection with her. Then I remembered my own words to my student—took a breath, and thought about being present. Immediately, the mare breathed too and settled down. I had a good laugh at myself, and a gratitude moment for the student who reminded me to 'stop the chatter!'

So how do we become 'present'? I use three simple steps that anyone can do. They are: *Breathe, rebalance your body,* and *expand your awareness.* Breathing should be slow, deep, and calm. Rebalance means simply to check our position in the saddle. Expanding awareness is about using our complete, 180-degree peripheral vision. In other words—lift and relax your eyes and look around you! Whenever I get lost in a horse's issues, I just go back to these simple reminders, and we reconnect without using force or stressful riding. Of course, no one can keep this going every moment. The good news is, we can refresh these simple steps as often as needed. As Sally Swift would say: "Find it, feel it, let it go."

After this reminder to myself, I take a breath, expand my awareness, and Trucker settles down and is moving nicely underneath me. We work on simple exercises and transitions, and really begin to enjoy the ride. When I would lose my connection with Trucker, and 'busy world' came back, I would breathe and expand my vision, and we would be working together again. I repeat this as many times as needed, and gradually, I am present for longer at a time. Why would I want to waste a single precious minute of the lovely ride I can have on a good horse, just to live in busy world? As soon as I become aware and present—we are both happy and flowing together.

Karen and *Sammy*, connection through the reins.

Through the Reins

The mystery of contact.

The rider's connection with the mouth of the horse is a question that comes up at every clinic and lesson that I teach. When a student asks me how much contact they should have, my answer is always: "It depends." It depends on the age and stage of the horse's training. It depends on his physical structure and body issues. It depends on the horse's state of mind that day. Most important—contact depends on the rider's seat, balance, and freedom of movement in their own body.

The old masters that I knew would say: "The rider's hands are connected to the seat." In my earliest years of riding this made no sense to me at all! In those days I was still trying to fix each part of me as instructed: "Quiet hands! Keep your legs still! Look up!" When *Centered Riding®* and better awareness of the big picture came along, the *seat to hands* connection finally began to make sense. I learned that if I am centered and stable in the saddle, then my arms and hands are free to give and receive information from my horse.

The reins are for feeling the horse's
thoughts—not to control him. – KI

In my jumping days, my instructor often worked his students on grid exercises without reins. We were not allowed to hold on to any part of our horse so we learned to rely on our seat to stay on. When you are jumping through a long sequence of fences, you cannot pinch with your legs either, because you will be popped off your horse's back eventually! Those tough exercises gave me a very secure seat in the saddle. Because I was not dependent on my arms for balance, I was able to ride with following hands over the fences. My horses were light in the hand, never pulled, and were able to freely use the entire length of their bodies over the jumps. Since they were allowed to find their own balance, they were also relaxed and didn't rush.

This was trial by fire for sure! Many years later, in learning about the core psoas muscles and their use, I am able to teach my jumping students how to develop an independent seat in an easier way. In clinics, we play games to teach riders stability *off* the horse, and pair up with human 'horses' in partner games to learn how the horse feels. Tai Chi classes are another way of learning to be deep and grounded in your center, and have free and flowing arm movements. On a steady horse, while I am warming up in the arena, I still practice riding with the reins laid on my horse's neck, and do the slow motion, freeing arm movements of Tai Chi.

Notes from my journal:

Many riders try to control and 'set' the head of their horse, and drive the horse into gripping hands. This method blocks the horse's ability to balance and move naturally. Be honest with yourself—are you allowing your horse to move forward, is he truly stretching? Or are your hands busy trying to 'fix' him? I don't manage it every step, but I work on being honest *and looking always for softness in my hands, with my horse truly forward and stretching over his back and out his neck. Is he really reaching to my hand, or am I pulling backward to find his mouth? If he ducks behind the contact or drops his back and loses energy, then I know to **release** my arms (not pull more!) and ride forward. I give my horse a chance to seek the contact with me. This is the only way to have a happy, willing partner. Be honest, be willing to let go, be willing to give.*

So what about contact? I like to think of my arms as belonging to me, and my fingers to my horse. More specifically, I use my *ring fingers only* to connect with my horse's mouth. The rest of my fingers and thumb are soft and partially closed.

To achieve this, my seat needs to be secure and my arms hanging below my shoulders. This allows my arms to be free to move and give and my fingers can feel my horse's mouth and have a quiet conversation when needed. The amount of contact varies from horse to horse, ride to ride, and the situation. Some horses do best with a shorter contact in the warm up, until their backs can stretch and release. Others like a medium rein length at first, so they can work in a longer stride and frame.

Maddie, a much larger warmblood mare that I worked with, required a very long loose rein and a half hour minimum of relaxed walking warm up before she would ask for the softest of connections with me. My hotter thoroughbreds were best with a shorter connection at the beginning of each ride. They felt insecure if I was not clearly connected to them and they would rush and spook because they needed clear direction. Given time and patience, they would gradually relax, let go and stretch into a longer rein. Each horse is an individual, and every ride is different!

Bottom line (pun intended), the mystery of contact is about our seat in the saddle. With a balanced stable center, riders can let go of dependence of their hands and really listen to what their horse is asking for, in each moment.

Andy and I have just started our ride. We are alone in the arena today, soft music is playing, and with no distractions it is easy to join his calm mind and let go. He is my little Zen teacher, this horse. As I begin some easy circles and bending I can feel my seat melt into his back and the lovely swing of his body. His peaceful breathing encourages me to breathe calmly with him.

Oh so gradually, we work into other movements— serpentines, leg yield, shoulder in, haunches in— which help both of us become more flexible and supple. We take our time, and as Andy's strides grow longer and his back comes up, he begins to come into a shorter, rounder frame. I wait, taking up the reins in tiny stages as he offers them to me. If he needs to stretch out again, I release the reins back to him. It is a lovely, private conversation between the two of us. We know each other well, and I always listen and wait for his offers. Andy is generous and enjoys our rides, so I know that he will tell me when he's ready to move on.

When I feel him thinking about trotting, I let myself find the trot in my own body and he lifts me willingly. After a few soft circles and bending moves at the trot, there it is—he very gently stretches to my quietly waiting hands on the reins and oh so softly rests his sensitive lips in my fingers. It is almost overwhelming. His trust in me is truly a gift and I never take it for granted. Life is good.

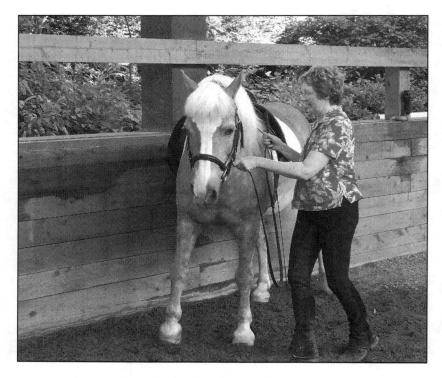

Groundwork exercises.

Slow and Steady

Interval training for the pasture potato.

From my journal:

Spring has arrived! Andy and I are just getting back to work, and taking it slow and steady after our winter break. I am fully aware that working too much, too soon, with a soft horse, can lead to problems. The lessons I learned from my event coach about interval training are remembered!

Before I mount up, we start with some in-hand work at a walk, bending and suppling moves for Andy, a few slow trotting circles on line, and some stretches for myself as well. When we have both loosened up a bit, I get on Andy with music by Ronan Hardiman playing on the arena speakers. It is perfect riding music—flowing and lovely, and it is easy to let my body go with my horse and the music.

I have no plan or agenda, just to get myself centered and in good alignment so that Andy can balance himself underneath me. I let the music fill my senses and open my breathing while I wait to see what 'horse' I have for that day. Riding on a medium long rein I check into my position: Are my seat bones even? Is my lower back released? Is my head balanced and my neck free? I begin to feel more lift and swing in Andy's back and suddenly we are totally matched and in time with the music. The feeling is one of being completely present, in each moment. Andy and I are connected because I purposely did not 'train' or push, I simply allowed time and space for this to happen. By making our warm-up about me, the rider, there is no pressure, and my horse is calm and relaxed.

We are both nicely warmed up and connected now. I begin to ask Andy, very gently, to lengthen his back a little more, add more energy, and take longer steps. The music helps us stay in rhythm and not rush. I simply release my lower back, bring my seat under me a bit more, and breathe with intent. Andy will usually respond with longer steps and lengthen his back. If I want a bit more energy from him, I use a light, forward 'brush' with my lower legs, left and right, in rhythm with his movement. Then I sit quietly with the movement that he offers. If he slows again, I repeat the same aids, or add a light tap with a crop if needed. This is a better and kinder way than using stronger leg aids, kicking heels, and nagging every step. Aggressive aids just create a tight, resistant horse who will end up dull to your leg. My goal is for my legs to feel as if they are floating on my horse's sides. He appreciates this and has learned to move forward when I ask lightly and then release my legs.

We add some leg yields and bending circles—always looking for flowing energy and purity of the gaits. I check into my own position frequently so that I do not get involved in 'doing' or forcing any movement. Once Andy is forward, bending, and connected to my hands, I begin to play my 'picking up the reins' game. Very gently I shorten the reins just a bit, in small increments. If Andy loses energy then I brush, brush forward with my lower legs and release my elbows slightly. When he steps into my fingers with his back up and swinging and neck extended, I very slowly release the reins, keeping the energy and the connection clear yet soft. The release of the reins is my 'thank you' for his acceptance of my hands. If I repeat the ask and release, over and over—I will have a horse that is always willing to step into my fingers with a soft, forward, and happy connection. He learns that I will let go as often as I ask, so he is happy to give.

We continue to play the rein game like an accordion – going from a shorter and rounder frame, to a longer, more reaching frame. If I am clear and consistent with my aids – then Andy rewards me with wonderful flowing movement that sings like the music that is playing. This is the true gift – a happy horse, in self-carriage and lightness.

In order to receive, we have to be willing to give. – KI

Never underestimate the value of a great walk session in training! It is a real workout for an out-of-condition horse to carry our weight and use their body correctly. Many riders don't take time to develop the walk, which is the most important basic gait in training. Without a good walk—the 'fancier' moves you do later on will not be correct. In this session, *Andy* was 'breathing' when we finished, but not stressed, something that I was taught to watch carefully. I pay attention to my horse's breathing and increase his work in small increments when he is ready. We always end our sessions with a walk on a long rein for cool down and reward.

Interval training with horses means riding for alternating periods of walk, then trot, then walk, and repeat. You can gradually increase the trot work and decrease the walking times as your horse's fitness improves. When he is ready, add periods of canter in between trotting and walking periods. Watch your horse's breathing, respiration, and recovery time on the walk breaks as a check on his fitness.

It is also good to mix up your routine. For a horse coming off a long break, I will spend the first few weeks riding mostly at the walk, hopefully in and out of the arena, with some easy trotting work every few days. A longer more intensive ride one day will be followed by a shorter easier ride the next day, or a relaxing trail ride at the walk. Riding over ground poles and using cone patterns once or twice a week adds variety and interest. So put on some great music, enjoy riding the basics, and your 'Pasture Potato' will be sound and fit in good time!

Riding Light

Lessons from down under.

SOMETIMES WE GET LUCKY and opportunities come up that help us turn a corner in our riding and training. One of those moments, that I especially remember, was meeting an Australian who had come to the States to teach for a few months. On a whim I went to audit one of his clinics and I learned some valuable lessons. David, the instructor, was a very successful three-day event rider and he was applying his Aussie style of riding and training to a group of dressage riders. This was right up my alley, with my jumping background and new interest in dressage. I had not yet met Sally Swift or heard about *Centered Riding®*, so my idea of dressage at that time was to ride with too much leg into too much hand. In those days, this was the current method of instruction. I had no idea that things could be any different. A weekend watching the Australian changed all of that!

From my journal:

> *This weekend, I audited a clinic with David Westmore from Australia. He is an amazing three-day event rider with the most flowing ability over a fence that I've ever seen! He demonstrated with several horses and worked with groups of riders too, so that I was*

able to come home with a clear idea of his techniques and style. The horses in the clinic were all upper-level dressage horses and he blew our minds away by having everyone ride in half seat, or light seat, on a longer rein. His theory is that most riders spend too much time, muscle and effort on over-collecting their horses. When he demonstrated, he rode each horse in half seat, folded slightly in the hips, and up off the saddle. David didn't work on a lot of bending and flexing or fancy tricks. He simply let the horses move forward and stretch out. When he got on each horse, he would warm up at a walk, and then go right into long trotting, cantering, and galloping in light seat. Something not really seen on 'fancy' dressage horses!

David's style was a real shock for the tradition-alists. His point—we need to refresh the basic gaits and let our horses move out and extend their bodies. The long extension muscles of the horse need training also, to balance out the shorter collecting muscles. Basically, he was teaching cross training to dressage riders. The horses loved it and the difference in their movement afterward, when David brought them back to do a bit of collected work, was amazing. They had more lift, more energy, much better engagement, and a beautiful freedom in their way of going. Best of all, every single horse showed a happier attitude.

I went home from the clinic eager to try this out on my own horses. At the time, my most advanced horses were a thoroughbred gelding and an Appaloosa stallion that I had raised and trained for jumping and dressage. After my years of jumping, riding in half seat was natural for me. It was fun to rediscover this lighter style after the almost too vertical dressage seat that I was being taught at the time.

Roman, the thoroughbred, immediately responded to the opportunity to lengthen his frame. On our first ride after the clinic, I spent twenty minutes riding him really forward in the three basic gaits, with me in light seat position. We finished with a free rein cool down at the walk. The next day we went on a relaxing trail ride, and the following day we did another session of riding in half seat. On every ride, I made sure to give *Roman* enough rein to lengthen his body, yet still have a very light connection, like working in a longer 'rainbow' frame. I kept this up for two weeks, with a day off once a week. By the end of the two weeks, *Roman* was moving through his entire body, totally released in his neck, and swinging with happy rhythm. It felt like he was ready for the next step, so after another warm up in half seat at all three gaits, I picked up the reins just a bit, changed my body to be slightly more vertical, and there he was! Engaged behind, rounded in the back, and connected lightly to my fingers on the reins. His collected movements and lateral work were like floating! It was truly an important moment in my training.

With the stallion, *Ghost*, this method was just as effective. He had a completely different build than the longer bodied thoroughbred—he was shorter coupled, more 'up' in front, and thicker in the neck. Collection had always been easy for him, but lengthening his shorter frame, not so much. After two weeks of doing the same exercises with *Ghost,* he was able to really extend his trot and canter, yet still be balanced and light. His already nice collected work got even better. As a bonus, after the forward riding sessions I ended up with a horse that was happier and more willing to listen to me. Stallions do not like to be over-controlled and they prefer an equal partnership. Training one requires you to be respectful, clear, and fair. *Ghost* appreciated being given

Karen and *Ghost.*

more freedom to move and he responded by connecting with me on a higher level.

Since meeting David, I have been using his methods with all of my horses. Once or twice a week, I like to work the horses in half seat only, up off their backs, and really let them move. Twenty minutes of this is plenty, with some walk breaks on a long rein, and a free-rein cool down afterward. The horses love these low key 'play days.' It keeps them fresh, forward, willing, and happy. This is now a regular part of my cross training routine. Try this out yourself. Shorten your stirrups a hole or two, pick up a half seat position, and let your horse enjoy a good long trot or gallop. Fun guaranteed!

Being in Partnership

Enjoying the ride.

D EVELOPING A PARTNERSHIP WITH A HORSE (or any being), means letting go of agenda and being present every step of the ride. This is how we can truly enjoy the journey. Otherwise, we keep putting that future goal ahead of where we are at **now**, and we will never feel good about our rides, nor truly connected to our horse *in each moment*. Being present is the only way that we can effectively influence our horse's balance and movement. When we ride with agenda and expectations, instead of being present for each moment, we are putting stress on our animal partner. This stress is often more than we goal-oriented humans realize.

Invite your horse to play with you!
– Cathie Madden, A.T.

"Reward every try" is something you will hear from many of the natural horsemanship trainers. It is a good reminder to ask ourselves if we are truly living by such a simple code when we work with our horses. Trying to get something done when a horse is not ready is an abuse of power and privilege. All beings learn more in a positive atmosphere with a reward-based teacher, rider, or handler. We are much more willing to try again if someone says: "Yes! You are getting it!" (And then hands out the cookies!)

Riders are often shocked when I suggest they leave their goals at the gate and just simply enjoy their ride. Goals can cloud the gift of our animal partner's generous efforts to please us. Each effort is a micro step on the journey. And the more present and patient we are, the quicker we get there.

From my journal:

I was sitting in the stands at a clinic taught by Steffen Peters, who is an internationally successful dressage rider. The students were all top-level competitors on stunning and talented horses. One rider had a very hot, sensitive horse and asked Steffen if he would get on her horse and work on his piaffe. (Piaffe is the trot in place—a very difficult and advanced movement for a horse.)

Steffen got on her horse and rode him along the wall, halted, and asked quietly for the piaffe. He had no whip or spurs by the way. The horse absolutely exploded! Steffen never moved in the saddle, he just waited for the horse to calm down and stroked him gently. Then he walked the horse along the wall, halted, and quietly asked again for the piaffe. This time the explosion was half as much. More waiting, and again, the stroking. Steffen stayed calm and never reacted to the horse's emotions. After several more tries, with quiet patience on Steffen's part, the horse happily offered a lovely piaffe and calmly halted. It was an amazing example of a rider knowing that his horse was trying, and giving him time to relax and find the movement being asked of him.

Less truly is more, and the longer I ride, train, and teach—this simple truth becomes one of my most important life lessons. I have found that the *less is more* philosophy affects everything I do in my life. In our busy, demanding days, we often get stuck in 'get it done' mentality. When I slow down, I see that I have accomplished enough and had time to enjoy it along the way. Working with my sensitive horse, my dogs, or my students reminds me to leave spaces, watch with kind eyes, and be patient. Time and maturity have taught me the following:

Real learning happens in the spaces we leave. It happens in the release after the 'ask' and in allowing the try. This is the gift of being in a truly balanced partnership. – KI

Karen and *Andy.*
Photo credit: Epona Moon Photography.

And The Journey Continues

The true nature of a student.

YEARS AGO, I WAS SITTING WITH ONE OF MY ELDER riding teachers, a very wise man, who was adored by horses. At that time I was beginning to realize that I could often 'hear' what the horses were saying and feeling. If I told anyone, they laughed. "Horses don't talk!" they said. So I learned to keep quiet. But on that day with my old teacher, I found the courage to ask him if this was really happening, and could everyone hear the horses. He replied: "Not everyone is listening." I remembered this only recently and I feel so grateful for his answer. This story is important because I think everyone who loves animals should know that, yes, we can ALL hear, if we are listening.

Being with horses is about more than just riding them. It is about *Life*. It is about the Big Picture of Life. It has taken me many years to see beyond the details and the end-gaining goals I had in my earlier days. Going from the simple happy kid with her horse, to the years of hard work and competing, to seeking a real partnership with my horses—has been a long and winding journey. To find the joy and fun again with horses has been like coming full circle and finding those magical moments where I feel like a kid again. But now, I have the addition of experience and maturity, and a better understanding of my four-legged friend. I know that he has more to teach *me*, than I have to teach *him*.

Learning can be difficult for many of us. It is often an unfamiliar and uncomfortable place to be! We don't like to feel awkward or clumsy or ignorant. But as a teacher, and a student too, I know that real progress happens when I let go and stop worrying about looking or feeling foolish. We can be patient with ourselves about learning. We are not horses! We have to learn 'horse.' If we can let go of wanting to be perfect, then we will always be able to learn and keep growing.

> ***Be willing to be confused. Be willing to not know. This is the true nature of a student.***
> ***– Tom Nagel***

These days, my goals, such as they are, are very simple: to be with my horse or dog partner in the most fair and positive way possible. That means putting ego and 'wants' aside. When I am with a horse I get *quiet* so I can hear; I *wait* for the horse, and *reward* every try. If I give my horse time, then he will offer again and again. This is the way to finding the real *dance* with our horses. And as I grow older, this *way* applies to every part of my life, with all beings, on all levels.

My best to you, my friends, on your own *way* and on your own journey!

Photo credit: Epona Moon Photography.

In Appreciation

THE ORIGINAL IDEA FOR THIS BOOK came from Tom Nagel, and I am grateful to him for his encouragement and assistance throughout this project. To Sue Ennis, who brought me a copy of Tom's book, which opened so many doors. To Sally Swift, of course, for changing my life on every level. To my spiritual teacher and friend, Carol 'Nokomis' Bearss, who was the first person to help me really see and hear the beautiful nature around me. To Barb Apple for generously sharing her amazing horsemanship skills. With much gratitude to Dr. Mary Jane Mack for her care and support in keeping me healthy and balanced. To Elizabeth Mitchell, for taking care of my horse, *Andy*, during my years of travel and teaching clinics around the country. Also, to the many wonderful teachers I have had on my journey for their patient instruction. And, especially, to all of my students who have learned, laughed, and shared along with me. (You all know who you are!)

Special thanks to Jeanie Wier of Epona Moon Photography for her beautiful photos; to Barbara Clark for her drawings; Robin Dorn for permission to use her illustrations; and to the students and friends who allowed me to share their stories.

And, of course, much gratitude goes to all of the wonderful horses who have been my teachers.

Drawing by Elizabeth Mitchell.

SOME GOOD READS

Centered Riding by Sally Swift

Equine Fitness by Jec Ballou

In the Company of Horses by Kathleen Lindley

The Tao of Pooh by Benjamin Hoff

Zen and Horseback Riding by Tom Nagel

Andy.
Photo credit: Epona Moon Photography.

Made in the USA
Lexington, KY
21 September 2019